of such things.

of such things.

Poems

ESTHER KAMKAR

ZIBA PRESS

2018

Copyright 2018 ©
Esther Kamkar | Ziba Press
All Right Reserved.

ISBN: 978-0-9967056-4-6

Acknowledgments

Cover art by the author Esther Kamkar.

Epigraph on Page 1 – Excerpt from "The Layers" by Stanley Kunitz (1905–2006) from The Collected Poems of Stanley Kunitz, Copyright © 2000. Reprinted by permission of W.W. Norton & Company, Inc.

Poems on Pages 63–65 – After the twelve questions in *The Vertical Interrogation of Strangers* by Bhanu Kapil.

Poem on Page 66 – *Tao Te Ching* by Lao Tzu, Translation by Stephen Mitchell. Copyright © 1992. Excerpts reprinted with permission of Harper Perennial, imprint of HarperCollins Publishers.

Poem on Page 102 – Title from Richard Diebenkorn's "Painting Guideline #8" in a list of guidelines the artist wrote that was seen at an exhibition at the De Young Fine Arts Museum, San Francisco.

Poem on Page 104 – *Crow Mother and the Dog God: A Retrospective* (Pomegranate Catalog) by Meinrad Craighead. Copyright © 2003. Excerpt reprinted with permission of Pomegranate Communications, Inc.

Previously Published

Portside.org
"Song of Drone" April 2015; "Over There" February 2016; "Where? Where Are You going?" October 2017

Distrumpian Almanac.org
"Keyhole" "Pulses" "Whatever the Sea" May 2017

For my mother
Monireh Sharim
and my grandsons
Rocco P. Parry
Luca P. Smith

CONTENTS

Part 1

5   Talking to Myself
7   Fire Blossom Earth
8   Thorn Bushes
9   Red Earth Black Earth
10   Ruin Lust
11   Preface to "This Poem is a Ruin"
13   Flame Eater and Acrobat
15   You Live under My Eyelids

Part 2

19   The Light and So Much More
20   Seaweed Seaweed
21   Bread Water Flowers
23   Whatever the Sea
24   A Living Dark
25   He Will Be a Geode, Not a God

Part 3

29 Pulses
31 Remembering the Earth
32 Provisions
33 What is a Harbinger?
34 Gossip of Bones
35 Sar-é-Sang, Afghanistan
36 First Gift
37 Honey Thief
38 Begging Call
39 *Morir Soñando*
40 After Aristotle's Lagoon

Part 4

43 My Mother Sings
44 Approaching Simple
45 Rehab Sequence: Wheat-Barley & Knit-Purl
48 Birds Fly into Windowpanes
49 In the Autumn
50 Bus Stop
51 The Gate

Part 5

57 Somersault
58 Thirsty Wool Colors Crimson
59 How will you begin?
60 Where did you come from / How did you arrive?
61 Who are you and whom do you love?

62 From Writings on Lao Tzu's *Tao Te Ching*
66 Postcard Poems: Wish You Were Here
68 Cylinder Seals

Part 6

73 Silence (What Remains)
75 Speech Pathology
77 Natural Intelligence: NI
78 Where? Where Are You Going?
79 Katrina Didn't Like To Be Lonely
80 Striptease
81 Over There
82 Grief Sees No Borders
83 Keyhole
84 Song of Drone
85 Crossings
86 This Must Be A Mistake
87 A Bone, A Feather

Part 7

91 Waiting for a Poem
92 Releasing Birds
93 Solitary
94 Puzzle Pieces
95 Your Story
96 *Keep Thinking about Pollyanna*
97 Ghazal: Tonight
98 Harvest

The Layers
Stanley Kunitz
(1905–2006)

*How shall the heart be reconciled
to its feast of losses?
In a rising wind...*

*In my darkest night,
when the moon was covered
and I roamed through wreckage,
a nimbus-clouded voice
directed me:
"Live in the layers,
not on the litter."*

POEMS

Part 1

Give me a threshold,
an entrance.

Talking to Myself

Poetry is for getting rid of fear.
    Fear my enemy. Fear my friend.
    My canary in the dark mine of the mind.

We must recover and uncover our memories. A country without memory is a sick country.
    I thought something was lost, lost in this room. I should
    have searched the rest of the house, but could not remember
    what was lost. I have everything I need.

Bury me standing. I have been on my knees all my life.
    Is a Romani with no country, without any memory
    of the WW II Devouring, a sick Romani?

When in doubt, sauté onions.
    Stand barefoot in the kitchen; soles of your feet sprout roots
    as you peel and cut red, white or yellow onions.
    Bring in onions by the bushel on your day of Festival of
    Doubts.

Let there be work, bread, water and salt for all.
    I saw a man and a woman last night, dancing on the roof.
    Dancing and weeping. Dancing and weeping.

My father was a miniaturist, pleased with all the small things of life.
>   I speak to dusty green olives on the tree:
>   Shiny black olives
>   I'll pick you one by one and cure you.
>   It would take us forty days to cure each other.

An image is stronger than a song, a morning song.
>   How to measure the roughness of the world
>   in the Valley of Seahorses?

Fire Blossom Earth

When its fire steals all air from my lungs
I go to the nursery to humble and to hold
The fire-breathing dragon of the mind
Feet on the floor of the heart
Eyes assenting to grief.

Do plum petals want the earth
As much as it wants the blossoms
In this cycle of giving and receiving?
You stay here to breathe.
Do not follow me home, Monster.

Every house has a kitchen
I roll tangerine-sized chickpea
Flour and cardamom meatballs
Between my palms. I stand
Alive and intimate with my pea-sized
Monster, cooking.

Thorn Bushes

Thorn bushes
Spring up
Wherever
An army
Passes and
Thorn bushes spring up
In the hearts of
The passing
Army

In this war
Of love
Long
As the pregnancy
Of an elephant
Darkness
Gives her
Radiance
Because she
Lets it.

Red Earth Black Earth
after Shirin Neshat

silk flower tree is dizzy

words penned
on my skin something
about using my hand
and then the cowards
deluged me fingered
my body to gouge
the words
clandestine dissent

logic of birds

in detention devil's beloved
cracked my bones scrolls
filtered deeper

waves of dancing skirts

solitary
behind doors
the codes penetrated
to the marrow

women's enclave

obscured veiled
forbidden unspoken
words I swallowed
cemented with the light
of the moon

Ruin Lust

We didn't want to visit ruins
stayed with relics in our own domestic landscape.
In the kitchen I was slicing persimmons into petals,
could hear him mumbling, as if over a coffin.
When did I begin feeling phantom pain
for my missing ear, my lung?

I remember the courtyard of his chest,
ruin's decay a memory of perfection.

Preface to "This Poem is a Ruin"

Slow-tongued, I struggle
with words and with diction
in the underground tunnel.
I brush against the chiseled
walls of alphabets, not only
the alphabet of childhood
the song of the language
and its syntax. I learn the word
for perturbation in another language.
I hold the torch tightly as the water
rises to my knees.

Maybe it is easier to return
to the Periodic Table of Elements
and to start with Gold for a dome
Silver for sage and my hair
Mercury for the heat
Zinc for healing the wounds
Iron for the splint on my tongue.

And when the *sadness of shoes* from a dream
stands with me between the Hall of Names
and Facing the Loss, I fold a crying
stranger in my arms. Contours of absence.
Mute ash. When did I become everyone's mother?

What to do with the remnants that line up
under: What survives in the dryness of desert
after two thousand years?
Black braid, wooden comb, dried fruits
leather sandals, bronze ladle, thirst
of wells, whispers in the sand.

Not a hoard of gold coins found
in a dig, but these:
The salt of longing rises from the sea.
Wind, the conductor of the wadi.
Red ripe mulberries by the rhyming
inscriptions on tombstones.
Give me your hand and your winter.

Again from a dream: *my hand on the door handle*
is in every door. I exit and I enter
I escape and I infiltrate
in/out   inside/outside
in-between   crossing the threshold.
What is on the other side?
The older-self having a forty-year old
conversation with a younger-self?

How to bring in the fence that is not a fence,
it is an iron and concrete wall between checkpoints,
soldiers with guns and people waiting to cross.

Which of the eight city gates will let me in
into the poem? I cannot be arrogant
with such things. I say:
Gate of Mercy, have mercy on me,
and wonder if clarity is expected.

Flame Eater and Acrobat

Flame eater and acrobat
moor their maroon canoe
at the harbor and unload cargo.
They set up their tent
and start work among us again.

The flame eater juggles torches
by the roadside.
I say:
> Come with me and make this door
> beautiful for me to enter.

The female acrobat, standing on her hands
on the sand, looks up at me.
I ask about her friend, the woman
who walked on broken glass without bleeding.
She says:
> She turned into a glass shard and went to sea.
> She'll return to the shore one day
> a red nugget of sea glass, if you look for her.

I speak to flames:
> Give me a handful of hinges and doorknobs.
> Eat this door.
> Give me a threshold, an entrance.

I speak to oystercatchers hopping on their long red legs:
    Teach me happiness,
    how to want only
    the oyster, not
    the pearl.

And to the toss and tumble of the sea:
    Make the jagged edges smooth.
    Make me glass.
    Make me glass.

You Live under My Eyelids
    for Barbara

A tiger slips in
A high-wire girl slips out.

I see magicians, flame-eaters, bears,
Miniature chairs; I send them to you

Under my eyelids.
I know what you love.

The elephant sprays water on flames
And you say: Love extinguishes the pain.

What to do with your mermaid from Ixtapa?
Do you still have a sea in your eyes

Under your eyelids?
Squash blossoms around your neck,

You are an émigré in a floating world
Where everything keeps changing forever

From new to old and even older
Where tiny boats journey past each other.

Part 2

The open flowers
are easy to pick.

The Light and So Much More

You sent me cadmium red
and green-gold, I wore them
on my breastbone.
The slow hydrangea bloomed
at last, and the stars in the night's
pocket taught me how to bend
to the bitter and the sweet.

When you are not here with me
my eyes search for you
at every door, waiting
for your arrival.

You arrive and your pigeons
form in the air to follow you:
Passenger without a suitcase
a man with lips that remember
the softness, the brush and clasp
of a lover. You see me before I open
my eyes to see you.

Stare at me for a while, like the hawk
that perched on the fence,
looked straight into my eyes
before it flew away.

Seaweed Seaweed

Like Sargassum she is free-floating, drifting
without any firm point of attachment

She listens for the sounds of Sargassum
when she utters its name

"Sargassum" and hears whatever sound-waves
gather around her—

saga sage grass sugar
argument mass aggression

grass sum sage argument
saga aura egress retreat

departure escape exit exodus
means of egress

point of no return
assume argue float

Unmoored, undulating
to shrug off the weight of her aloneness

Bread Water Flowers

1
My mother taught me to never step on bread.
I pick up the piece of bread and kiss it,
before I place it in a safe corner
away from trampling feet.

I save all the pencils I find on the ground.
I keep a pencil for Ashraf, who could not write,
her palms were bloody and swollen. I keep
a pencil for Behrouz, whose fingernails
were ripped out. And one for the poet
Farrokhiyé Yazdi, who could never read
his poems, his lips were sewn shut.

2
When I left my childhood home
at eighteen, they poured water behind me
to symbolize light and a safe journey.
My father wrote me for many years
started his letters:
Dear Light of My Eyes.

3
Every summer-end, my mother sent me
to the rose garden to fill my skirt with rose petals
for making jam. The open flowers were easy to pick.
I watched and waited for the rosebuds to open for me.
Sometimes they did, and sometimes they didn't.

Whatever the Sea

Time doesn't pass, it curves around us.

I am the best person to transport you

I do it by touch, you say in my dream.

I mistake your hand for my own, holding the pen

I reach to take the pen and write for us

Push the boat out, whatever the sea

A Living Dark

In that terrible passage between the touch
of the sun and one particular visit,
the old things were given to a neighbor
for safekeeping, before the lineup
and transport.

Delicate hand-embroidered sheets
and pillowcases, with no memory
of skin, were someone's dowry.

Something of the personal glows
in the darkness behind those old
things. They go on without
that someone, that lonely one, no one.

He Will Be a Geode, Not a God

Where is he in the Milky Way,
with galaxies, black holes and quasars
swirling in his head tubed to a ventilator
and brain shunt?

His fragility is his strength
as a fragile infant is powerful.

In Persian, there is a single word
saayeh for shadow and shade
>   *May your saayeh*
>   *be over your children's*
>   *heads forever.*

Good for his wife to have someone to love,
to record doctors' diagnoses and treatments
in the ICU, to transcribe into an email every night,
to make a shopping list of what he loves:
Persian cucumbers, black tea, and the Gypsy Kings.
It is good to have someone to love.

His fragility is his strength.
Devastation of earthquake nourishes the Earth.

Part 3

This is a gift,
not a riddle.

Pulses

If Archimedes were here watching the marble heads
each on a round white piece of cloth, floating
between rafts, undulating without falling
in my dream, he would have dipped his fingers
in water and tasted them.
I would have held his wrist between
my fingertips to read his pulse.

Choppy   Throbbing
Deep or Shallow
Thready   Hesitant
or Scallion Stalk

This is the International Year of Pulses
in which pulses are feasted upon and praised
for feeding us, and giving back to the earth.

Chickpeas are pale pulses
Lentils green and brown pulses
Split Pea   Cowpea   Dahl
Fava Bean   Bambara

There is another husk
in which all through the year we measure
the pulses of the fallen and the drowned
of the world.

And yet another in which we set each other's pulse racing.
The underside of our wrists longing to be touched.

Remembering the Earth

Taste of earth in my mouth, digging a tunnel to China.
Sitting cross-legged on dirt playing marbles with pebbles.
Jumping in puddles, muddy earth pushing up
not swallowing me down to the dark depths.
Chalking a hopscotch, sliding the flat stone, jumping
the squares, hoping not to land on the half-moon of hell.
Silver markings on soil, snails' message: the holes in sage
and borage leaves are our work, be back tomorrow night.
Adam of red earth, red like blood, wheat from the ground
for bread, king and beggar together in a lump of clay.

Squeaking new shoes for the New Year in spring bragging
to budding pansies and hyacinths in the inner courtyard.
The tap of tiny pebbles on gravestones in a cemetery the color
of lions saying goodbye to grandparents and brother.
Sifting the earth through a sieve, mixing with water from a toy
samovar for miniature mud cakes, for a pretend bite.
Fortune-tellers excavating the basement for gold coins,
echo chamber, Alaska and Eskimo bars melting in the mouth.
Garden snake creeping upon the path, the gardener sending me
to the kitchen to bring bread and salt, a peace offering on dust.

Provisions

If you come back and you are as I remember
smelling of eucalyptus under the sun

I'll say yes, this time.
If you come back

in your silken vest with no memory
of the lone cypress, I'll still say yes.

If you never come back, for the rest
of your life, I'll be ready with wine

and sweets for when the time comes,
for going to the orchard and telling the bees.

What is a Harbinger?

Then, I had nothing,
only a bag and a knife,
no roadmap, or signposts,
no idea what is
a harbinger of what.
Landmarks were places
I got lost.

Now, at harbor
I still have a bag
and a knife.
Vulnerable
as if my fontanel
is a funnel, as if
it never hardened.

Gossip of Bones

You say:
>A groundless rumor
>not the truth.
>The exiled to the island
>were only dogs.

I say:
>You herded
>and disappeared
>us too.

I say:
>Salt water
>Skeletons

You say:
>A groundless rumor.

I say:
>We were the backbone
>of the city.
>Look at the stone buildings
>we built, the moldings
>and friezes:
>plaster, acacia gum
>ground bones.

You say:
>Mere gossip.

I say:
>The flesh was yours,
>the bones are ours.

Then, I rinse my mouth,
spit out silkworms.

Sar-é-Sang, Afghanistan

Nuggets of lapis-lazuli grief,
dense blue pendulums, dowse
for fugitives in the kingdom
of ginkgo and longevity
as legions of envoys
suspended in longing,
and transitions,
resisting the fantasy
of completion toil
in the blue mountains.

Glint of fool's gold exists.
Eternity and caves exist.
Gravity exists.
Blood exists.

First Gift

Where did all his sweetness come from?

She cups her hand as if holding honey
and walking with it, like Samson.

This is a gift, not a riddle.

The first bee cleaved and scoured
the emptiness of the lion's carcass.

Honey Thief

With what tenderness you swathe and hold.
With what swiftness you spin your tales
to distract, and deceive like a magician.
Your old wound is still raw.
Honey won't heal it.
After prison you can't sleep in rooms
with closed doors, you say.
Do you keep the wound open
like a door to perform magic tricks?
Who is the storyteller
speaking with your mouth
embellishing and conjuring
the offices of other worlds
and different kinds of remembering?
For the thrill, or for hunger,
it is safer to steal my honey
because your hand is the twin of my hand.

Begging Call

Mockingbird's
loudest repertoire
wakes me with you
on my mind. Heartbreak.

June heat in your city
our escape to Paris.
L'Oiseau Bleu
of my harlequin heart.

Morir Soñando

So, I gave you my eyes to see
milky-orange delicious
Morir Soñando;
to die as you dream,
to die as you sleep,
a hall of colors
under your eyelids:
Snowflakes
Picasso's dove
Orange peel
Ibis
Wild iris
Persimmon
Saffron
Houses in Oia
Apple flesh
Flames.

After Aristotle's Lagoon

After two cicada-life-cycle years
you heard my voice
and found me in Covent Garden.

I was no longer mute.
I was with wings.
I was singing.

Part 4

We are traveling
together as a family.

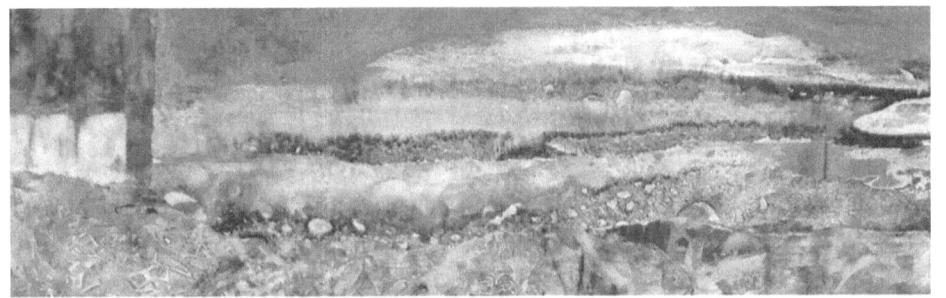

My Mother Sings

As she steps down
the stairs counting
one-two-three

before her foot finds
a solid surface again,
my mother remembers
and tells me the story
how she ran from rooftop
to rooftop with her cousin,
Maryam, eighty-five years ago.

I use coconut oil
to massage her swollen
legs, it improves memory
I have heard. Gold filigree
cardamom pods necklace, red blouse,
flowered skirt and velvet leggings
is what she wants to wear,
and I help her.

She listens to world news
on her shortwave radio: BBC, VOA
VOI in Persian, as we play rummy
and backgammon. She calls
the cards, and the dice to win.
She smokes a second cigarette
in the evening only when her heart
narrows with melancholy.

She sings to her oldness.
She forgets she is hungry.
She is my toddler for a week.

Approaching Simple

Approaching simple
Staying small
Nevertheless
Never the more

My mother in the hospital again.
At home, I wipe the avocado-smeared high
chair as I listen to my daughter crying-laughing
her news on the phone: It is a boy.

Bittersweet. Watermelon shavings, my mother's
remedy for high fevers, and for weak stomachs
egg yolks beaten with sugar.
She has pneumonia again.

The courtyard house of my mother's childhood
on my mind, not to fill the chambers,
but to stage a sort of housewarming.
A passage.

We are traveling together as a family.

Rehab Sequence: Wheat-Barley & Knit-Purl

    1.
They are sending me to Rehab to kill me.

    2.
Where am I?
She closes her eyes
as soon as she hears Rehab.
Her hair doesn't stand up
like in the barber joke my brother
told us. I lose my hair, she says.

    3.
Mr. R. almost as old as my mother
in his wheelchair, bargains
with a visitor the fare for two
passengers and two suitcases,
for his caregiver and himself
to escape.

    4.
Mr. R. starts keening at 7 pm
in the lobby every night, waiting
for his pills:
"Maman, Maman, give me a cup of tea.
A cube of sugar, Maman."

    5.
She has no need for a gauge
to measure distances.
She swims effortlessly
from Sea of Dreams to Sea
of Memory to cards in her hands
to win another game of rummy.

6.
Aloe Vera's wet flesh sooths her skin.
Bring fruit and tea for everyone.
My mother on the wheelchair
sings in her dream:
I love you, you love me…

7.
Purl-knit: barley-wheat field is a selvage.
Short hallways are long walks.
Turn off the stove and the lights.
Lock the front door before you sleep.
Her mother hen-ness is awake and solid.

8.
The nurse must have found someone
and is making love somewhere.

9.
The red Joker card brings laughter.
Knit-purl: inbreath-outbreath
So far, so good, she says.

10.
The Egyptian woman wrapped
in a woolen shawl the color of rust,
wheels her chair closer to me,
rubs the baby blanket between her fingers.
Her blue eyes smile.

11.
They don't need a room
for lovemaking, the staircase
is good enough for them.

12.
In the lobby, by the Christmas tree
Mr. R.'s wife feeds him with a teaspoon
"No more, leave me alone!"
His son shaves his father's face
with an electric razor.
TV commercials blare out of Room 1.
I knit my white baby blanket
sitting on the couch between my brothers.
This could be a scene from an Italian comedy
with Nino Manfredi, I tell them.

13.
Barley-Wheat   Knit-Purl
On my lap the baby blanket
grows to a heap of sugar
sprinkled with confetti.

Birds Fly into Windowpanes

My mother is my child for a week.
She is present like a sheaf of wheat.
At ninety-five she is like a toddler sometimes.
She drops her Kleenex everywhere.
Her left eye has tunnel vision.
Her right eye is blind.
How is she not anxious, or afraid?
I marvel at her memory for old poems.
I scrub her back in the shower
        the softness of her skin soothes me.
Euphemia changes her clothes.
My mother tells her You are my daughter.
My mother tells her You are my boyfriend.
She whips raw and cooked egg yolks
        with olive oil to make mayonnaise.
I check her breathing every night.
In her sleep she reaches out to catch a child
        before falling, one of her ten.
I wait my turn to enter.
I wonder who will care for me when I am old.
Children? They can break your heart.

In the Autumn

I phantom-dry persimmons in my mind,
pretend to simmer quince, sugar and bruised
cardamom pods in a copper pot
I brought from Ireland—the vendor at the farmer's
fair claimed *pure Irish copper, lovey!*
as I nodded yes, and read the Persian name
of the maker below an etched lion—
quince steaming, the lid wrapped in a towel to make
rosy-red jam, the color I imagine my mother's
sealed lips as they grew into a rose blossom
in her dream, for good words only
to come out of her mouth, she said.

I seed an imaginary bushel of pomegranates
to chill in a blue bowl, as my good childless aunt did
as she waited for us to come home for lunch
wishing she was our mother.

I fancy growing sugar crystals on a string
to promise as a gift to the poet—with closed eyes I open
the Divan of Hafez to read a ghazal
to divine an answer to a *beautiful question*,
then ask for permission by offering a branch
of sugar—before reading the following ghazal,
the interpretation.
They say Branch of Sugar was the name
of Hafez's beloved.

I liked to make things in the autumn.

Bus Stop

All around the outside of Brentwood Manor
at the corner of Santa Monica Boulevard
& Wellesley Avenue, between 7-Eleven
and the big blue bus stop, the residents drink
at 7:30 am from coffee cups, cans of beer,
cartons of milk, and share cigarettes,
and day-old donuts, tease each other
and laugh. A young man offers
me an empty bottle of rum.

They sit on the bench to rest, not to travel.
Like Stumbling Stones on sidewalks of Berlin:
they make me trip, they make me think
of their cribs and toy dump trucks.

Waiting for the #1 bus to the hospital
I'm standing between my old
mother and my grandchild to be born,
holding my breath.

The Gate
Pechakucha for my mother

[Light]
Her name Moneer, from the root of noor, light,
anar, pomegranate, related to Anwar, related
to ner, candle, in Hebrew & menorah, candelabra.

[Enemy]
She said: I think all the boys and girls of the world
are my own. I pray for them, I pray even for our enemies.
Who are our enemies? I asked.
Ourselves. When we don't listen to the words
of our heart we become our own enemy.

[Shoulder Pain]
Starting from scratch
picking the leaves, stuffing, folding,
wrapping, stacking, simmering for hours,
lifting, dividing fairly for each household.
Her favorite was the top layer,
the hard boiled eggs in their brown shells
infused with the scent of grape leaves.

[First Born]
Appendicitis was the cause of his death
at seven. Her sisters-in-law mocked her,
their young bride, saying:
the eggplant also boasts its child
to be the fairest of all.

[Namesake]
We laugh and accept the obvious
that her favorite child is our oldest brother,
one of her nine. We understand.
We are all parents now.

[Belly Button]
Why are you hiding your belly buttons?
The new fashion is exposing them, She told
my teenaged daughters. Men pour wine
and sip from their beloveds' belly buttons
in Persian poetry, she said.

[American Army Jacket WWII]
In her dream my father stands in the river
wearing the jacket he bought in Tehran Bazaar,
extending his hand to take hers.
He is young, coaxing her to follow him.
But she turns away.

[Plums]
Immobile in bed she whispers:
Your father just left
to bring me cheese & plums.
He promised to come back to get me
Where is he?
Now I'm ready to go with him.

[Sugar]
Still a luxury in her mind
she asks us to take the sugar cubes home
after the tea and fruit of her imagination
are served to visitors at her bedside.

[Loquats]
Years ago, when we were denied permission
to pick a few loquats, wild forest pears,
from my neighbor's tree, my mother said:
He must have suffered from hunger in his home country,
not enough food for so many people.

[Calendar]
When a nurse asked, does your mother know today's
date and the year, I prickled: The Islamic calendar
year, Hebrew, or Western —
and it was in the fair order of things
when she clarified the hospital uses only
the American calendar.

[GPS]
I held her hand and spoke loudly into her good ear
It's me, Esther. She wanted to know which Esther.
Your Esther, I said. And that was good news to her.
She was checking her mental GPS, and knew
she was on this side with me, not on the other side
with her aunt Esther.

[Water]
Then she wanders into a story
I cannot decipher, but I wander with her,
we swim effortlessly from the Sea of Memory
to the Sea of Dreams, and to a sip of water
from the straw.

[First Thanksgiving]
Her ESL teacher asked: Do you know what turkey is?
Did you eat turkey in Iran? She had no idea,
did not know my mother's recipe for the stuffing:
Rice, pistachios, saffron, dried apricots & rose petals

[Eighth Great-Grandchild]
She wished my daughter, the birth-giver,
an easy delivery: May her limbs open
in goodness.

[Half]
She said When are you going to take me home?
Take me home with you!
And that— that in particular—
broke all of us in half.

[Camel]
Death is a camel sleeping
behind everyone's door, she said.
No one knows when it will wake up.

[Rose Water]
In the middle of the day, she escaped to the street
to sit on the curb, as was her plan. We offered her
white orchids, splashed her with rose water.
At the end we left her there all alone.

[Cooling Earth]
She always said giving the body to the guardianship
of the Earth cools the grief.
Witnessing the finality of loss, she meant, and she was right.

[The Gift]
After fifty years, I have lost
the fear of losing her.

Part 5

When it rains be human.

Somersault
after Edmund de Waal

I don't risk a chance to pass my feet
over my head, to turn a somersault
any longer, an upside down blood-rush
breath pause breath turn silence.
But late-arriving words just parade
in a backward way, settle themselves
alone or in clusters like porcelain vases
on shelves, where breath is held inside
and between each vessel, between the words
and the page as they perform somersaults
and finally stand perhaps with a twist in the air
before landing, or with an awkward angle
as feet steady themselves and tremulous breath
turns and returns. When words swinging
deliriously don't mean only what they stand
for, but the strangeness gleaned from the air.

Thirsty Wool Colors Crimson

Arid land, her body
Withered fields, her skin
Reservoirs drained
Lakebeds shallow
Parched groves, cracked
Like her lips
Wells run dry
What if it just never
Rains again
A longed-for deluge
Or even beads of dew

How will you begin?

Eve of Summer Solstice
Here is the river
The air is fragrant
with tiny strawberries
There
are the redwoods:
Cinnamon-colored bark
Only I seem not to know
there are no birds' nests on the map
Here is the compass rose
The planet tilting towards
the Sun
How will I know if my ladders
go up, or down?
No peace in my ignorance

After the twelve questions in *The Vertical Interrogation of Strangers* by Bhanu Kapil

Where did you come from/How did you arrive?

it marks you   your birthplace
home of childhood
traveling outward from Mother Tongue
with or without dictionaries
to write in another language
means embracing its foreignness
and marrying it
to talk about foreignness
is like talking about love
and the confusion with articles
and prepositions and punctuation
keys to enter meaning
lowercase/uppercase letters
don't they sound the same?
words and dreams in an adopted language
for moments I read documents
laughter matters
not color of quince flower, but peach-pastel
how a handful of grain
can signal joy
how one word can stand
for milk faucet lion
how in spring you may find
a spring by a spring
and say this word also
means the eye of the Earth.

After the twelve questions in *The Vertical Interrogation of Strangers* by Bhanu Kapil

Who are you and whom do you love?

At times an expert
on myself, remembering
my toddler son's words—
I'm hungry, sometimes I'm mad
and sometimes I'm a giraffe.

Sometimes, I am tangled
in confusion.

Am I not a mountain?
Am I not layered and brittle
like shale?
Desert-thirsty, longing
for the absent.

Surely a deserter,
as grains of sand
quicken and fall,
how I neglect to turn
over the hourglass
of my heart.

After the twelve questions in *The Vertical
Interrogation of Strangers* by Bhanu Kapil

From Writings on Lao Tzu's *Tao Te Ching*

6.
It is always present within you.
You can use it any way you want.

What do I want?
I want not to want
The possible and easy
The impossible
A new book
The best brush
A leopard in my pocket

19.
just stay at the center of the circle
and let all things take their course.

Imagine a woman, who entered
The circle, took her place in the center
And remained.
For balance she spread her arms
And legs, like da Vinci's
Drawing for proportion.
In that stillness in the center
She thought of sea foam and jam
Foam in her kitchen.
Sea foam, jam foam
Full of air, not much substance.

20.
Stop thinking, and end your problems.

Like a bird, swooping down
Making a nest, doing her work
Unafraid of the possibility of a footstep
Unworried about a flood, or floods of the past
Or the cat who took her eggs
She comes and goes each year
Doing her life's work
Without fear
Without worry
Without regrets
Without thinking
Without problems

23.
Express yourself completely,
then keep quiet.
Be like the forces of nature:
…when it rains, there is only rain.

Don't pretend to be all and everything.
When it rains be human.

33.
If you realize that you have enough,
you are truly rich.

I have a mermaid in my dreams
I have two mothers; one is myself
I have white stones and black stones
I have pages and pages of writing
That amount to nothing, except
My own sense of belonging to the
White page
I have a hummingbird; she writes my poems
I have old baggage on the carousel
I recognize it and smile, but don't
Pick it up.
I have a pomegranate tree in my garden.

35.
When you look for it, there is nothing to see…
When you use it, it is inexhaustible.

How can you think
You are not beautiful
And deserving
Of this moment?

36.
If you want to get rid of something,
you must first allow it to flourish.

After reading Chapter 36
I don't need to forgive
Myself one thousand
Times a day.

55.
…the power is in this.
He lets all things come and go
effortlessly, without desire.

My life
Is effortlessly
Full of desires
My desires
Have wings

Postcard Poems: Wish You Were Here

No. 1
When you said
I'm glad
you're out there
in the world
I imagined
you saying
I'm glad you're
here, your hand
on your chest.
Right here.

No. 2
This is the house Tagore lived
in the year he was 18, at his window
the sky turbid, the light lacking luster
like a dead man's eye, he wrote.
Such loneliness and longing
for the eye-kissing light of Calcutta
for his mother, for India's salt.

No. 3
Honey, barley and wheat beers
Soaps with potash and oils
Indigo-dyeing of wool
Recipes on clay tablets
in Cuneiform.

No. 4
Herdwick   Suffolk   Swaledale
Roughfell   Cheviot   Blueface Leicester
Ryeland   Texel   Blackface Northumberland
the sheep in the center is the one
my deaf poet friend in Cumbria shepherds.

No. 5
Agatha Christie's favorite tools:
Face cream
Orange stick
Fine knitting needle
to scrub and polish five
thousand ivory carvings
her husband dug up in the three
thousand year-old ruins of Nimrud
near Mosul, before they shipped
them to London.

No. 6
Paula Rego's muscular woman
or a man in drag?
You have to hurt the dog
to give him his medicine—
is the title of her print.
Cruelty and tenderness.
Like a wind coming through
the door sideways, a dream
makes you think of other things.

Cylinder Seals

*King Ashurbanipal crying before Ishtar,
the goddess of fertility and warfare
like a child asking his mother for help.*

[Description of the carving on a 2"x 1" Mesopotamian stone cylinder seal at the British Museum]

Chalcedony

I didn't go looking
for my childhood home
but to Keats' bedroom
his parlor
not my childhood home

Obsidian

In the hushed halls of treasures
I whisper over and over:
You belong to Persia
Go home to Greece
You must be in Egypt
Go home to the one who loves you
I whisper

Black Serpentine

Dancer on the Dark Dark Sea
watches over me
the venom in my belly
Cormorant cares for the wound
watches over me

Marble

Underside of your wrist
endless sugar
This Body Real as You See Me /
That Body Real as I See You
endless sugar

Granite

No roadblocks, no soldiers
with guns, only low drystone walls
enclosures for sheep along the South Tyne River
Sheep like white buttons on green hills
drystone walls, wild geraniums, buttercups

Green Serpentine

An ibex, or a scapegoat
turning one hundred-twenty turns
going home to Scarberry Hill
to Hawthorne and the one-eyed pet lamb
in silence, in silence?

Garnet

My concertina heart unfolds
I copy Nephin's cone on the cover
paste Sheila's hummingbird on page one
glue the children's horses, collage
the Aga stove, an elephant
My heart unfolds

Lapis Lazuli

Something so simple, so small
a sunflower seed
a hill of ten million porcelain seeds
glazed in black with white stripes
I leave them, walk by the river
something so simple, so alone

Carnelian

I didn't go looking for a mapmaker
to make me a navigation map
Squaring the Circle
is an ancient unsolvable problem
my map is the shape of things

Part 6

in the mouth of one poem.

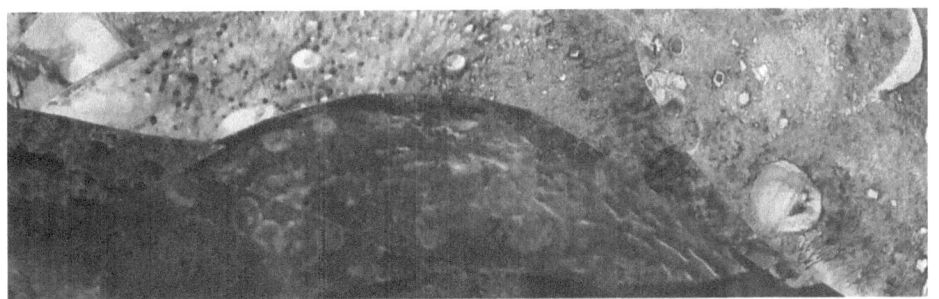

Silence (What Remains)

Boat
Sea
Sea
Sea

First I see the whale on her sweatshirt,
and think she is on a whale-watching boat
in the Pacific Ocean where it mingles
with the Salish Sea, waiting for the orcas
to leap out of the water.
No! She is on an unseaworthy
wooden boat
crammed in-between people we know
not their names, we call
them migrants and refugees.
Someone has tied her shoelaces.
I wish her dry land.

Refugees
Migrants
who are running to get there —
How do you keep your blisters clean?
How long can you carry your child
on your shoulders as you run
and walk?
Did you bloody your back crawling
under the razorblade fence at the border?

Forest
City
Train station
Platform

Ticket
Passport
Wait
Back on the bus
Refugee camp
Wait

Where do you wash your baby's bottle?
What words do you use to comfort your children?
Who do you feed first?
Have you had your period since you left home?

You are running still.
I am still silent, listening
to catch the rattle and whimper
of your house keys
in your pockets.

Bread and silence
are for breaking.
What remains?
Shoes.
Always shoes.

Speech Pathology

is not flaws in:
phonation
        articulation
                fluency
                        resonance
                              voice

it is a language disturbance:
        Absurdity of the conjunction of words—

Give birth to the bomb
Nuclear scientist's Postnatal Depression, after explosion
Missile's umbilical cord
Oppenheimer's Baby
Hiroshima's Little Boy
Radioactive decay process as a Daughter Product

The language of death is banished from Death making—
Not killing people, but collateral damage
Not incinerated, but carbonized

Speech pathology is not in:
                stuttering
                      lisping
                            lallation

It is not:
    aphasia
        echolalia
            echolalia

It is in MOAB, Mother of All Bombs.

Baby Moab was born to Lot and his elder daughter after Sodom's destruction.

        conjugal
            conjugate
                conjunction of words

Natural Intelligence: NI
[AI can compose music and write poetry, 2017]

like a dictionary
open the body
to its Cat's Cradle page
make Ace of Hearts
make Candles
remove string, tighten the loop
make another figure
make Cradle
I say, let's be lovers
like Okiku and Yosuke
and Play Cat's Cradle
let's make House
let's make Breastbone and Ribs
let's place pillows in the chambers
of our hearts to console
someone, at least one.

The Lovers Okiku and Yosuke Play Cat's Cradle, a painting by Eishosai Choki, 1804

Where? Where Are You Going?

Don't leave your home.
Don't cross thresholds and borders.
The boats are bottomless.

Even if the sea does not swallow you
and you find dry land,
your heart will be broken.

You thought the softness
of your flesh would protect you.
You'll be lost in the crowd of foreigners.

You'll be a no one, a number
in their eyes, cool with mistrust.
Your high cheekbones won't remind
anyone of your grandmother's
and your name stripped of its meaning,
pebbles on the tongues of strangers.

You'll lose your ground.
Grammar of the new language will riddle
your bones, hipbones and spine
won't align to sit on earth.

You'll long for the scent of jasmine and bread.
You'll miss the gold fish in the garden.
You'll forget the names of trees and flowers.
You'll lose the key to your house.

There is no refuge, no sanctuary.
The boats are bottomless,
vessels to extermination center of the sea.

Stay where you are,
where you know the color of the hills
in winter, spring, summer and fall.

Katrina Didn't Like to Be Lonely

She rolled in to have a good time
to dance to the foot-stomping
infectious rhythm, to touch
every thing and every one.

She came to be with people
face to face, to dazzle breathless
with her spinning powers.
She loved them all, the old

and the young, egrets, roofs
lawn chairs, street signs, palm trees
anhinga wings, Labradors
broken flowers, carnival dolls.

She hurried to find
a place to plant her feet.
She was traditional.
She was pure circle.

Striptease

Unbutton your coats.
Shed your scarves and belts
and watches.
Prepare to disrobe.
Empty your pockets.
Surrender the keys
to your precious
belongings.
Undress.
Spread your legs.
Raise your arms.
Husk yourselves.
But first you must take
your shoes off, as if
you are entering
a mosque for prayers.

Over There

My Zuni friend says:
They burn people over there,
they just burnt a pilot last week.
They are talking to us.
They want to tell us something.
They want to tell us that they know our history:
How the Indians were killed over here.

How the Indians were burnt in groups of thirteen.
First they were hung, toes barely touching the ground,
then wrapped in hay and lit on fire.
Twelve for the Disciples, and one for Jesus.
He says:
They are talking to us, they mean
to tell us that they know our history.

Grief Sees No Borders

Grief sees no borders,
it enters our bodies.

Smell of burnt flesh and hair, blood
the same color in Fallujah, Aleppo
and Bamako, same number of bones
in shattered skeletons in Paris.

My ribcage grows a new rib
to hold my heart in place.

The boats are falling apart,
the children are sinking.
They are all sinking
in the Mediterranean Sea.

The sea absorbs them without
prejudice, and without empathy.

The children are sinking,
each one of them knows
how to eat a pomegranate
without losing a seed.

Keyhole

The ways we miss our lives are life.
    Randall Jarrell

I want to reconsider the possibility
of consolation. The bereaved mother
accepts the gift
of dates and coffee
offered by the soldier's mother
    Let her in. I want her here.

When will we arrive in the country of longing?

No matter the wreckage
this is what we have now.
The door is lit by a keyhole.

Song of Drone

Targeted strikes conform to the principle of humanity.
    CIA Director John Brennan
    Attorney General Eric Holder

What I love most are weddings and funerals.
I feast on one so I can feast on the other,
for days I wait in song.
Am I a honeybee, or a bagpipe?

An angel, or a dragon?
Above all things a flying dragon of hellfire
and a blessed light of the divine, an angel.
Why are my eyes so big?

To taste the foods spread beneath me to feed
a never-ending appetite for the delectable animals,
vegetables, minerals, plastics in motion, or rigid
like tombs I mark, double, or triple tap to strike.

My intentions are transparent, my patience legendary.
I hover and watch for weeks, like a *zamurah*
piper in the marketplace waiting for a glimpse
of his *burfi*-sweet beloved.

The fire in my belly launches in a gentle
hiss to ignite the celebration
to decimate and devour the caravan of delicacies.
Smoke rises to greet me.

Crossings
after VERSschmuggel

It is possible
to smuggle a poem across the border
to entrust rhythm and melody to ears
to surrender sense and syllables
to confide fragments from mouth to heart

It is possible
to abandon the avenues of one alphabet
to forget the names of trees and flowers
to trade alabaster for gypsum
to wonder was it the wolf who ate the grapes
to cross the border as a mourning dove

It is possible
to put two tongues
in the mouth of one poem

This Must Be A Mistake

This must be a mistake.
Addressed in invisible calligraphy,
my luggage with a broken zipper,
was meant to be lost
with all its contents:
Foreign coins sewn in the lining
Keening of reed flute
Black rose of longing.

Her luggage
was her two-year old brother
in her six-year old arms,
feverish, when they crossed
the border into Texas.

A Bone, A Feather

Tiny charred corpses of sparrows,
Finches.
Who could have imagined:
The birds were burning.

Thousands of people
Tons of rubble
Thousands of watches
Thousands of pictures in frames
Thousands of rings
Thousands of shoes
Thousands of eyeglasses
Other images and other ghosts
Crowd in and confuse me.

The only way I can
Fit this enormity into my heart
Is to make it small
Make it smaller.

One woman
One man
One child
Smaller and smaller
A heart
A liver
A paperweight
A bone
A shopping list
A feather

Part 7

between our hearts

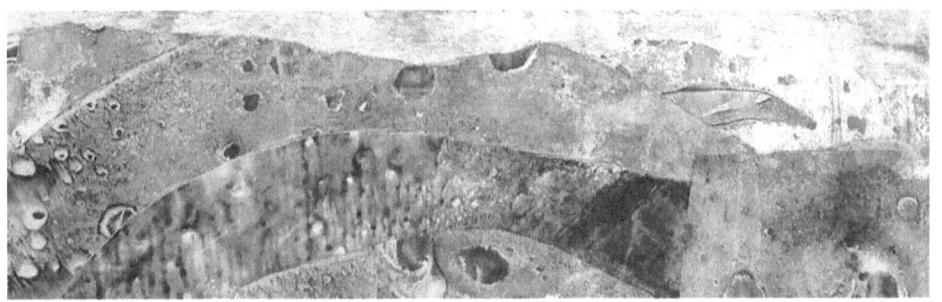

Waiting for a Poem

I'm waiting for a poem
something like a gasp
at finding a body
on the ground
behind the backdoor
and saying Stun me fear!
A poem with a museum
heart, its wings filled
with collections
of paper and clay
primeval.
A poem that ends
with no apology
for the possible sin
of living small.

Releasing Birds

I slept last night in a room
where someone died.
The birdman.

I dreamed of mud swallows
returning to their ancestral
shore to build their nests
remembering its particular mud.

Releasing birds with the birdman
was an illusion, as was shedding masks
with the camouflage man before him.

I redraw the contours of perception.

     Now it is morning
there is news of forty dead tiger cubs
in a Buddhist temple.
I remember the gift of the body parable:
to offer one's own body to save another.
My friend says any place with forty dead tiger cubs
is not a temple. My mind sends me erroneous
news bulletins: tiger-roars of my longings.
The birdman's fluid gestures
were for the birds.

Solitary

Some bees are solitary
Wild bees No colony No queen

They nest in hollow trees, stems of dried bramble,
snail shells: Red Mason bees Harebell Carpenter bees

Lavish pollinators No pollen basket No sting

The female bee chooses to lay a female, or a male egg.
The male bee protects the flowers, so she can eat: Lambs ear nectar

In the first cell, she lays a single egg on a ball of pollen and nectar
Then she makes a partition and builds a new cell for each egg.
Red Mason bee caps the entrance to the nest with mud.

Bee houses Bee condos Bee hotels: I fantasized
escaping to motels on weekends without my small children.

She leaves enough food for each egg, but never sees
her offspring as bees.

No honey No wax Solitary and wild

Puzzle Pieces

As she went about burying the crow
all she could remember
was her own young self climbing trees.

She found the dead crow at the edge
of the baseball field, outside the fence.
No crows circled above, no caw-caw

grieving ceremony under the white clouds.
Sycamore trees shed their leaves,
shed bark in jigsaw puzzle pieces.

She dug a hole, made a shoebox coffin.
She loved making things.

Your Story

You run home
with treasures
—leaves and figs—
in the upturned hem
of your shirt.
Once upon a time
there was a king
who had no money
—begins and ends here—
you must imagine
the rest. Bags of coarse
salt, a crown, walls
covered in feathers.
The story is clothed
in silence, passion
concealed in
the architecture
of tears and masking
tape. No lights lace
through the darkening night.
Impossible to unlock
the secret. Black rips
the page.

Keep Thinking about Pollyanna

How can you sleep at night?
Don't pretend such innocence,
the husband said with contempt.

She was not pretending.
She was a Pollyanna, had no idea
what was brewing in the basement.

She was not suspicious
of his silences, or the jar of metal on glass
from the loud mouth of the cellar.

She didn't see it coming.
How did I end up like this?
The wife asked herself, no one else to ask.

With goose bumps of longing,
I used to listen to Villa-Lobos'
Bachianus Brasileiras No. 5.

I lived on Glenn Gould's
Goldberg Variations scoring the stone walls
and sheepskin-covered floors

in an old house on a mountain.
How did I end up like this,
in a house without music?

From Richard Diebenkorn's "Painting Guideline #8"

Ghazal: Tonight

Six ladders lean towards six directions tonight
The black bear with coral heart-line is awake tonight

Like a body fighting to reject the new heart
They berate me; but I am staying here tonight

When I put my heart in front of the mirror
It multiplies: you are my mirror tonight

No more wishing, wanting and longing
We will disturb the wild things tonight

Our feet planted in the mud, our heads to the skies
Floating lotuses, spreading leaves, dancing tonight

All the yellow in Neruda's heart and tornado clouds
fused into a beam of light, shining tonight

To find the Milky Way, Esther is not leaving her house
The whole universe reflected on the ceiling tonight

Harvest

I pick the persimmons.
He picks the figs.
We fill the basket
with purple salvia
and hold it between us.
We eat a fig
we eat a persimmon
from the basket in the space
between our hearts.
Of all the voices this year
I love Meinrad Craighead's the most.
She said, *O Cave of the Heart*
illumine us, we beseech Thee.

About the Author

Esther Kamkar is a poet and visual artist living in Palo Alto, California. She published *Hummingbird Conditions*, a letterpress chapbook printed by Peter Koch Printers of Berkeley, California, through an Artist Grant from the Peninsula Community Foundation in 2001. Through her imprint Ziba Press, she published *Hum of Bees*, a collection of her poetry in 2011. Her poetry has appeared in anthologies such as *Let Me Tell You Where I've Been: New Writing by Women of the Iranian Diaspora* (University of Arkansas Press, 2003), *The Forbidden: Poems from Iran and its Exiles* (Michigan State University Press, 2012), and *al-Mutanabbi Street Starts Here* (PM Press, 2012). In addition to her work in literary journals, she has given featured readings in the San Francisco Bay Area, Washington, DC, and Great Britain (England and Scotland). Kamkar also works in visual media such as monoprints, encaustic, and collage. This is her third poetry collection published through Ziba Press.

COLOPHON

Cover and interior pages designed by Robert Perry of Robert Perry Book Design and Dutch Poet Press.

Printed and distributed by IngramSpark.

Display and Body Text set in Palatino.

www.ingramcontent.com/pod-product-compliance
Lightning Source LLC
Chambersburg PA
CBHW020428010526
44118CB00010B/473